Children's Sermons For Special Days

Twelve Children's Sermons And Activity Pages

Julia E. Bland

CSS Publishing Company, Inc., Lima, Ohio

Dedicated to
Sam and Andy, the family engineers

Copyright © 2002 by
CSS Publishing Company, Inc.
Lima, Ohio

For more information about CSS Publishing Company resources, visit our website at www.csspub.com or e-mail us at custserv@csspub.com or call (800) 241-4056.

ISBN: 0-7880-1914-7

Table Of Contents

Introduction And Suggestions From The Author

These twelve sermons for children observe a special day each month of the year. As we celebrate these special days it is well to remember that each day is a gift from God and an opportunity to teach our children some wonderful biblical truths.

The sermon has an activity sheet to be copied for the children to each have one. There is a coloring side for younger children and word games and puzzles on the other side for older ones. The activity sheet is meant to reinforce the lesson.

Study the sermon so that you can tell it in your own words, using your own personality and with the needs of your local children in mind.

The sermon as given is to get you started. Be open to the Holy Spirit as he guides you to add your own personal observations.

If you need notes, make them small and tuck them inside your Bible at the page where you will be reading the Scripture. Open the Bible and read from it. Children need to know that what you say really is from the Scriptures.

Ask questions and allow time for the children to answer. This will get them thinking and involved, but children can say unexpected things, so be ready to guide them back to the subject.

Before the worship hour, clip the activity sheet, a pencil, and crayons to a clipboard to be ready to hand to each child when the children's time is over.

As you pray and prepare, claim the Lord's promise in Isaiah 55:11:

> *So shall my word be that goes out from my mouth;*
> *it shall not return to me empty,*
> *but it shall accomplish that which I purpose,*
> *and succeed in the thing for which I sent it.*

May God bless you as you teach our children.

Julia E. Bland

A New Year
Each day can be a new beginning.

Scripture: 1 John 1:7b; (see also vv. 8-10)

Visual Aids: Paper and pencil with eraser

Handouts: Activity sheets

Advance Preparations: Copy enough activity pages for each child to have one.

The Sermon:

Do you like to make pictures? Something really fun is a *clean piece of paper, a pencil, and an eraser.

When we draw, it is easy to make mistakes. We might make something too big or maybe too small. Or perhaps our lines are crooked. A mistake is ugly and we want our picture to look nice. How can we get rid of mistakes?

We have an *eraser. Aren't you glad for erasers? We erase the mistake and do it over until our picture pleases us. We use our erasers at school, too. When we do our work there, we want it to be right.

We have a brand new year. Each day of our new year will be something like a clean piece of paper. The things we do will be on that day and sometimes we will make mistakes. Perhaps they will be big mistakes or small ones. We might not obey Mom or Dad as we should. We might not be nice to brother or sister as we should. We might not be as truthful as we should. Maybe we should have helped someone and didn't. Every one of us — you, me, Moms, and Dads — sometimes do things we shouldn't or maybe should have done and didn't.

This does not please God, and the Bible calls this sin. How shall we get those ugly things off our day?

We are sorry and we ask God for forgiveness and God washes them all away. What does God use to wash away our sins and forgive us?

Not an *eraser. Listen to 1 John 1:7b: "... the blood of Jesus his son cleanses us from all sin." This says it is the blood of Jesus that cleanses. We don't always understand how God works, but we believe he does what he says.

Of course we need to try to make every day a good one and try hard to please God with all we do. But a good thing for us all to remember as we start this new year is that every day can be a clean one even if we've done wrong. When we are sorry and ask, God will erase it all away.

*Use visual aids

Valentine's Day
Love binds us together.

Scripture: Colossians 3:12-14

Visual Aids: A large paper heart or heart-shaped valentine, four or more slips of paper with the name of a family member such as Mom, Dad, brother, sister, cousin, Grandma, Grandpa, etc. Or instead of the slips of paper use pictures. One or two paper clips. The heart shapes should be large enough to fold around the slips or pictures and paper-clipped together.

Handouts: Activity sheets

Advance Preparations: Copy enough activity pages for each child to have one. Prepare the visual aids.

The Sermon:
Do you like Valentine's Day? Is it fun for you to give and get valentines? What are valentines? Are they messages of friendship or love? What picture does a valentine use for the word love? Isn't it a *heart shape? Yes, a *heart shape is sometimes used instead of the word love.

There is a lot in the Bible about love, so in Sunday school and church we talk about it a lot. I am not talking about romantic love between a man and a woman who get married. I am talking about the kind of love all God's children should have for others. The kind of love that means we care that others are doing well. Let's hear what the Bible says in Colossians 3:12-13:

> As God's chosen ones, holy and beloved, clothe yourselves with compassion, kindness, humility, meekness, and patience. Bear with one another and, if anyone has a complaint against one another, forgive each other; just as the Lord has forgiven you, so you also must forgive.

This says that God's people are to show compassion, kindness, humility, meekness, and patience. These words mean that we are to care about others and help them and even forgive them if they hurt us.

Now verse 14 says: "Above all, clothe yourselves with love, which binds everything together in perfect harmony." Did you hear that? Love binds us together. Sometimes the hardest place to show this love is at home and with our family. Are *Mom and *Dad bossy? Is *brother a nuisance? Is *sister a pain? How about *Grandma and *Grandpa, are they sometimes grouchy? Does your *cousin tell on you?

Do all members of our family always agree? No, but if we show compassion, kindness, humility, meekness, patience, and forgiveness and if we truly love and care for others, arguments won't amount to a thing.

There is another family called our church family. Even here people don't always agree, but if we all show compassion, kindness, humility, meekness, patience, forgiveness, and love, then things will surely work out fine.

The Bible said love binds us together in harmony. Let's wrap this *heart which stands for love around these *people (slips with names or pictures) and fasten it all together. There, everyone is bound and held together with love. That is the best way to live and the way God planned.

*Use visual aids

Palm Sunday

Jesus wants to be king of our hearts.

Scripture: John 12:12-14

Visual Aids: A picture of the donkey and Jesus found on the activity sheet. You might like to color the picture ahead of time.

Handouts: Activity sheets

Advance Preparations: Copy enough activity pages for each child to have one. Prepare the picture of Jesus and the donkey.

The Sermon:

Have you ever seen a real donkey? Here is a *picture of one. In our country most people don't think much of donkeys. But, where Jesus lived, a donkey was a favorite animal. They were useful, too. They could carry people or heavy loads. Donkeys were animals of peace. If any king or his followers were thinking of war, a horse was the animal to use, but a donkey was used for peace. John 12:12-14 says:

> *The next day the great crowd that had come to the festival heard that Jesus was coming to Jerusalem. So they took branches of palm trees and went out to meet him shouting, "Hosanna! Blessed is the one who comes in the name of the Lord — the King of Israel!" Jesus found a young donkey and sat on it....*

On this special day we call Palm Sunday, *Jesus rode on a donkey into the great city of Jerusalem. There were many people in town that day because it was a special kind of holiday. These people had heard that Jesus could heal people, feed 5,000 people, and raise people from the dead. They were thinking, "We need this man for king. If he can do all that, he could lead an army, defeat and kill off the Romans who rule us, and make us our own nation again." ... Well, you know, Jesus loved the Romans, too.

But *Jesus was riding a donkey in peace. Can you imagine Jesus as a king on a horse leading people to war? Jesus didn't want that kind of kingdom. What he wants is to be *king in your heart and in mine.

Suppose for a moment that he had become their kind of king. He might have lived and ruled another forty or fifty years. Then what? He would never have been able to show us how much he loves us by dying for us. The world would have forgotten all about him by now, and we would be in a world without hope, never knowing God's love and how to love each other.

There would be no schools, no hospitals, no nursing homes available for everyone, rich or poor, because these things were started by people who knew how to love and care for others, just as Jesus taught.

There would be less good music and less great art because so much of our greatest music and art has been created and inspired by God's love in Jesus.

There would be no churches, no good life at all, and no hope of a life to come.

We are sad when we think of Jesus riding into Jerusalem to die on a cross, but we are very thankful he did.

*Use visual aids

Easter Sunday

Jesus promises us eternal life.

Scripture: John 11:25; 12:24; (see also 1 Corinthians 15:35-38)

Visual Aids: A package of seeds

Handouts: Activity sheets

Advance Preparations: Copy enough activity pages for each child to have one.

The Sermon:

Easter Sunday is a wonderful holiday for God's people. We celebrate the resurrection of Jesus. What does the word "resurrection" mean? It means Jesus died but he came back to life.

The holiday is so wonderful for God's people because Jesus promised that just as he was raised from the dead, so will we who believe in and love him be raised. Here is his promise from the Bible. John 11:25: "I am the resurrection and the life. Those who believe in me, even though they die, will live."

The same God, our heavenly Father, who gave us life to begin with can also give us life that lasts forever. There are things that happen in the spring that help us understand. Growing things come back to life when winter is over, like tulips, daffodils, and lilac bushes.

We plant seeds in the spring, and Jesus said planting *seeds helps us to understand resurrection. Jesus said in John 12:24: "Very truly, I tell you, unless a grain of wheat falls into the earth and dies, it remains just a single grain; but if it dies, it bears much fruit." When we plant a *seed, maybe a flower seed or the seed of something to eat, it must be put in the ground where it dies. But, when it does, a new plant comes to life and grows.

See these *seeds? Only if we plant them to die will they come to life and make a beautiful flower (or healthy food).

No one likes to think of dying, but we have this wonderful promise from Jesus that we will be resurrected just as he was. What does Jesus ask of us as he makes this promise?

He asks us to believe in him. That means believe he is God's son, believe what he says, and love him enough to do as he asks.

This is a happy day. Let's be happy!

*Use visual aids

Mother's Day

Jesus asks us to serve.

Scripture: Mark 9:33-35; 10:43-45

Visual Aids: Something mothers use when working, such as a potato peeler, dust rag, broom, laundry soap, etc.

Handouts: Activity sheets

Advance Preparations: Copy enough activity pages for each child to have one.

The Sermon:

This is a special day. What day is it? Why do we have Mother's Day? Is it to show our love and thanks for Mother or someone who is like a mother to us? What is it that makes Mother so great?

Jesus said something that will help us understand why mother are special in Mark 9:33-35:

> He (Jesus) asked them, "What were you arguing about on the way?" But they were silent, for on the way they had argued with one another who was the greatest. He sat down, called the twelve, and said to them, "Whoever wants to be first must be last of all and servant of all."

This tells us that the friends of Jesus wanted to be great, to be important. Jesus told them the way to be great was to be a servant.

Do you know what a servant is? A servant is someone who does things for others. Some servants do things for others because they have to or because they want to get paid. Jesus' idea of greatness was to be a servant because of love. Serving others because of love is Jesus' idea of greatness. Jesus proved his greatness by serving us in dying for us, and he did it because of his love.

Now, mothers are like that. They do many things, like *cook, *clean house, and *wash clothes. We could make a long list of things mothers do. Mothers do these things because they love us. They are being a servant like Jesus meant. Something else Mother does for you is pray for you. These are reasons why Mother is so special.

People who serve others are always loved and appreciated. We should all learn to be servants, helping one another.

We should show Mother our love and thanks often, not just on Mother's Day, but every day.

*Use visual aids

Father's Day
We listen to Father and obey him.

Scripture: Proverbs 4:1; 1 John 5:3

Visual Aids: A calendar turned to Father's Day in June

Handouts: Activity sheets

Advance Preparations: Copy enough activity pages for each child to have one.

The Sermon:
I'm looking at a *calendar here. It says this is a special day. What day is it? Yes, it is Father's Day. Today we honor and show our love for dads, grandfathers, or someone who is like a father to us. How will you honor your father? We can thank him for all he does, hug him, tell him you love him, and maybe buy or make him a gift.

This *calendar only shows Father's Day to be one day a year here in June. Should we honor our father only one day a year? Or, should it be every day? How can we honor him every day?

We can obey him — without a fuss. What are some things Dad might ask you to do? Help in the yard? Run an errand? Pick up toys? Be quiet and let him rest or read? Perhaps it is to listen when he tries to tell you how to behave. What does our Bible say in Proverbs 4:1? "Listen, children, to a father's instruction and be attentive, that you may gain insight." This is telling us to pay attention to Dad and do as he says. Then we will be much smarter.

There are many things we know our father wants us to do even though he doesn't tell us to every day. He wants us to be truthful, be kind, love God, become good citizens, and obey our city and county laws. He also wants us not to cheat or steal. Maybe you can think of other things that you know Dad wants you to do or not do.

We don't stop at love and obedience to Dad. We also show love for God, our heavenly Father, when we obey him. This is something every one of us should do. Moms, Dads, you, and me. Listen to what the Bible says in 1 John 5:3: "For the love of God is this, that we obey his commandments."

Let's make up our mind to obey Dad better — without a fuss! And our heavenly Father, too.

*Use visual aids

Independence Day
We pray for our country's leaders.

Scripture: 1 Timothy 2:1-4

Visual Aids: A U.S. flag

Handouts: Activity sheets

Advance Preparations: Copy enough activity pages for each child to have one.

The Sermon:

What do you think of when you see our *flag? Do you think of our country? We see lots of flags in July because it is the time we celebrate Independence Day, or maybe you call it the Fourth of July. We have fireworks and parades and a holiday. What are we celebrating?

We celebrate the time when our country's first leaders signed a paper called the Declaration of Independence. That means that this nation would no longer belong to England. Our people wanted freedom. This meant freedom to worship God as each thought they should. It means freedom to say what they thought, freedom from government interference in the lives of persons, and freedom to have our own government and laws with the right to change those laws if we wanted to. This paper said people had the right or freedom to have life, liberty, and the pursuit of happiness.

Those leaders of our country over 200 years ago did a good job. Most of them believed in God and they were trying to do a good thing. God surely helped them. They worked hard to make our country a good one. But today we can help our country, too. The Bible tells us how in 1 Timothy 2:1-4:

> *... I urge that supplications, prayers, intercessions, and thanksgivings be made for everyone, for kings and all who are in high positions, so that we may lead a quiet and peaceable life in all godliness and dignity. This is right and is acceptable in the sight of god our Savior who desires everyone to be saved and to come to the knowledge of the truth.*

We don't have a king, but we do have a president, vice president, governor, and others in government office. These verses tell us we are to pray for them all, even if we don't agree with them. Why? It says that we do this so that we may have a quiet and peaceful life, so that we can worship God, and so that all persons can hear the message of the Bible and learn to know Jesus as their Savior. The people in office need the guidance and wisdom that God can give them.

So, when you say your prayers, remember to pray for your country and your country's leaders.

*Use visual aids

School Starts

Jesus understands and will help.

Scripture: Luke 2:52; Hebrews 4:15-16

Visual Aids: A picture of a scroll from the activity sheet

Handouts: Activity sheets

Advance Preparations: Copy enough activity pages for each child to have one.

The Sermon:

It's time for school to start. Do you think you'll like it? School is work, but it's important to be in school to learn all you can. What do you think is best about school? Most boys and girls like to read. Learning to read is fun work and there are all kinds of good books. When Jesus lived there were no printed books like we have. Words were written by hand on *scrolls. The paper was made from a water plant or animal skins and rolled on two sticks.

Did you know that Jesus had to learn things just like you do? He was not born a baby knowing it all. He had to learn. He knows how it feels to be a child. He had to learn how to walk and talk, how to eat, how to study and have good manners. He had to do chores and get lessons done. As he grew older he learned from Joseph how to be a good carpenter. Luke 2:15 tells us how he was growing up: "And Jesus increased in wisdom and in years, and in divine and human favor." As he grew older, this says, he was getting smarter, too, just as you will when you go to school and learn all you can.

The Bible also tells us that Jesus understands and cares for us because he experienced the same things we do. Listen to Hebrews 4:15: "For we do not have a high priest [that's Jesus] who is unable to sympathize with our weaknesses, but we have one who in every respect has been tested as we are." Then we read in verse 16 that because Jesus cares and understands, he can help us. "Let us therefore approach the throne of grace with boldness, so that we may receive mercy and find grace to help in time of need."

When this says "approach the throne of grace," it is taking about going to God on this throne for the help we need. Jesus is there and he understands and will help.

Have you ever thought to pray and ask for help about school? Jesus understands and will help you.

Jesus also studied the Bible, as much as had been written at that time, and he memorized some good verses. We know because he often reminded people of what the Bible said. That would be a good idea for all of us to do.

Now, I have a question. Would you learn anything at school if you only went once a month or three times a year? No! It is just as important to come to Sunday school and church often. I'm so glad you are here today!

*Use visual aids

First Day Of Autumn

God keeps his promises.

Scripture: Genesis 8:22; Proverbs 30:5; (see also John 3:16; 14:23; 2 Corinthians 1:3-4; Revelation 21:1-4; John 14:15)

Visual Aids: Leaves from a tree, even if still green

Handouts: Activity sheets

Advance Preparations: Copy enough activity pages for each child to have one.

The Sermon:

September is a time when our season changes from summer to autumn — sometimes we call it fall. Do you like to see changes in weather? What will be happening to the *leaves on our trees? They will change colors and fall to the ground. Some places will have beautiful colors on the trees. Colors that almost look like jewels in the sun. They will be colors of reds, oranges, and yellows.

What season will follow? Yes, winter. Do the seasons ever get mixed up or one get left out? Does summer change to winter without the fall season?

Some things might disturb us like tornados, hurricanes, and earthquakes, but the seasons always come. How do we know they will? This is a promise of God here in Genesis 8:22: "As long as the earth endures, seedtime and harvest, cold and heat, summer and winter, day and night shall not cease."

God is dependable. That means God will do what he says. Some things or people are not dependable. We can't always count on people. They might not keep a promise. A friend might disappoint or hurt us. A job might not last. Someone's car might quit running or the electricity might go off. But we can count on God and his promises. Proverbs 30:5 says, "Every word of God proves true; he is a shield to those who take refuge in him."

The Bible has wonderful promises for God's people. There is the promise of his great love for us all and his gift of eternal life to all who will trust in Jesus (John 3:16). There is the promise of Jesus that he would be with us if we'll love him and try to live our life like he says (John 14:23). There is the promise that God is with us and will help when sad things happen (2 Corinthians 1:3-4). And there is that great promise of a home in heaven where life will be happy forever (Revelation 21:1-4).

We have a wonderful Lord! All he asks is that we'll love him, too, enough to do as he asks (John 14:15).

So, when we see the seasons change, we are reminded that God is always dependable. He keeps his promises.

*Use visual aids

Halloween
God sees our heart.

Scripture: 1 Samuel 16:7b; Psalm 139:23-24

Visual Aids: A mask

Handouts: Activity sheets

Advance Preparations: Copy enough activity pages for each child to have one.

The Sermon:

(Put the mask on.) How do I look? Halloween is a fun time. It's a time to put on a *mask and act funny or scary or different in some way.

I'll take it off and you'll see my real face again. But, my real face might be a mask, too, and so might yours — because you cannot see how I feel or what I'm thinking. Nor can I see the real you. We might look all right, but inside of us we might be sad, lonely, jealous, or angry about something. We can fool people, but we can't fool God. First Samuel 16:7b says: "... the Lord does not see as mortals see; they look on the outward appearance, but the Lord looks on the heart." This is a little scary because nothing is hidden from God. He who made us is able to see what's inside, if it is love or hate, kindness or jealousy.

But, it can be comforting, too, because sometimes we try to do something good and it doesn't turn out right or people don't understand. God sees how hard we've tried to do good even if others don't.

Knowing God sees our heart can be encouraging also. It can make us want to do good things, because we want to please our heavenly Father who alone sees how hard we try. And did you know we can ask for help? Psalm 139:23-24 says: "Search me, O God, and know my heart; test me and know my thoughts. See if there is any wicked way in me, and lead me in the way everlasting."

David wrote those words, and he asked God to look at his heart. If there was something there that shouldn't be, he wanted God to help him to know and lead him to do better.

We should try to have our hearts, our thoughts, our insides as beautiful or handsome as we like to look outside. This is possible with God's help, and it all starts with knowing Jesus as our Lord and trying to do as he says.

I hope you have fun with your *masks this Halloween, but remember God sees beyond your mask, your face to your heart.

*Use visual aids

Thanksgiving

Every day is a day for thanks.

Scripture: Psalm 118:24; Ephesians 5:20

Visual Aids: Thanksgiving decorations, such as paper turkeys or pumpkins, or use the picture on the activity sheet.

Handouts: Activity sheets

Advance Preparations: Copy enough activity pages for each child to have one.

The Sermon:

Thanksgiving is a happy time. It's a holiday and there is no school. Most people don't have to go to work. We think of *Pilgrims, pumpkins, turkeys, and fall colors. *Families and friends get together and have good times. We hate to see it end, but it does. People go back to work and back to school. Sometimes we eat leftover turkey for a few days and that reminds us that we had Thanksgiving Day.

For God's people every day should be Thanksgiving Day. Every morning is a new gift from God. Psalm 118:24 tells us: "This is the day that the Lord has made; let us rejoice and be glad in it." We could make a very long list of all we have to be thankful for, and it should begin with thanks for God's love shown to us in Jesus who died for us.

When we think of the good things in our life do we say, "We're lucky," or do we say, "God was good to us"?

Do we say, "We sure did something right," or do we say, "God helped us"? We know that the good things come from God and we should be thanking him. Ephesians 5:20 says: "... giving thanks to God the Father at all times and for everything in the name of our Lord Jesus Christ."

Let's try making every day Thanksgiving Day.

*Use visual aids

Christmas
Jesus came to show us God's love.

Scripture: John 14:9b; 6b-7a

Visual Aids: A photo of someone not locally known

Handouts: Activity sheets

Advance Preparations: Copy enough activity pages for each child to have one.

The Sermon:

Do you like December? It is an exciting time of the year. We decorate our homes, our towns put up lights, and we think of gifts. We have special Christmas programs, and we think of the time Jesus was born.

Many, many years ago before Jesus was ever born some people did know there was a God and that he was creator, powerful, holy, and fearful. Many did not really understand him as a loving Father who loves us all.

One of the reasons Jesus was born and lived here on our earth was to show us all what God is really like.

Look at this *picture. Can you tell from this picture what this person is really like? No. You can only see what the person looks like. To know what the person is like, you would need to meet him, get acquainted, and spend time with him. Then you would know by the way he acts, what he says, and how he treats others what he is really like.

This is what Jesus did. He came to show us what God is really like. In John 14:9b Jesus said: "Whoever has seen me has seen the Father." If Jesus loves everyone, then so does God the Father. If Jesus wants to help us, then so does God the Father. If Jesus loved us so much that he left his heavenly home to come and die for us, then so does God the Father. If Jesus forgives the wrong things we do, then so does God the Father. Jesus said there is no other way we can know God the Father except by knowing Jesus. John 14:6b-7a says: "No one comes to the Father except through me. If you know me, you will know my Father also." We rejoice and celebrate the coming of Jesus into our world to show us what God is really like.

*Use visual aids

Each day can be a new beginning.

Find the underlined words in the puzzle. They will go left to right or down.

When we do our lessons or draw a picture, we can erase any mistakes we make with an eraser.

As we live each day we might do things that are wrong. God calls this sin. If we are sorry and ask God to forgive us, he will erase those things away. The Bible says that it is the blood of Jesus that cleanses us. Each day can be a new beginning.

```
I  X  L  I  V  E  W  R  O  N  G
T  M  E  R  A  S  E  N  E  W  P
M  I  S  T  A  K  E  S  J  B  I
C  G  S  D  W  S  R  O  E  L  C
A  H  O  R  A  A  A  R  S  O  T
L  T  N  A  Y  Y  S  R  U  O  U
L  X  S  W  U  S  E  Y  S  D  R
S  D  A  Y  F  O  R  G  I  V  E
X  B  E  G  I  N  N  I  N  G  X
```

Help Bob find his way to school. Fill in the blanks with the letters he finds on his way.

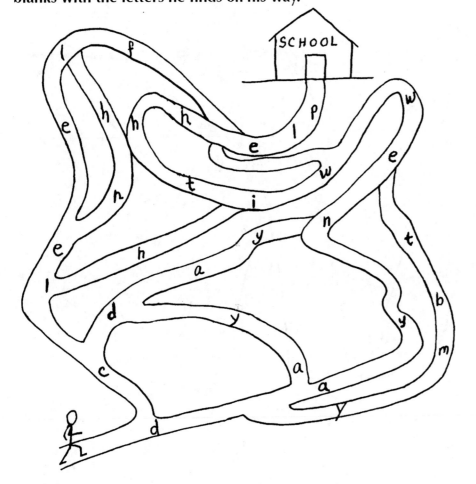

Across
Jesus shed his _ _ _ _ _
on the cross.

Down
He did this so that
our sins could be

_ _ _ _ _ _ _ _ .

... the blood of Jesus his son
cleanses us from all sin.
1 John 1:7b

Each _ _ _ can be a _ _ _ beginning _ _ _ _ God's forgiveness and _ _ _ _!

18

Love binds us together.

Find the words from the list in the puzzle below. They will go down or from left to right.

M	T	L	X	X	H	A	R	M	O	N	Y	J
E	R	O	H	K	I	N	D	N	E	S	S	E
E	Y	V	A	L	E	N	T	I	N	E	S	S
K	P	E	V	C	U	S	U	L	S	W	H	U
N	A	H	E	A	R	T	S	O	H	E	U	S
E	T	F	T	R	Y	A	I	V	O	L	M	T
S	I	O	X	E	X	N	N	E	W	L	I	O
S	E	R	Y	O	U	D	O	I	N	G	L	W
T	N	B	I	N	D	S	L	I	V	E	I	A
R	C	O	M	P	A	S	S	I	O	N	T	N
Y	E	T	O	G	E	T	H	E	R	X	Y	T
F	O	R	G	I	V	E	O	T	H	E	R	S

valentines   patience
have   forgive
hearts   live
stands   harmony
for   binds
love (2 times)   us (3 times)
care   together
others   Jesus
doing   wants
well   you
show   to
compassion   try (3 times)
kindness   meekness
humility

Draw a line from the word to what you think it means.

compassion   to not be proud or think yourself better than others
kindness   patient, humble, gentle, and not bossy
humility   sorrow for someone that is hurting
meekness   to have trouble without complaining
patience   to be gentle and helpful
forgive   to all agree and get along well with each other
love   a great caring and concern for someone
harmony   don't hold a grudge, give up feelings of anger

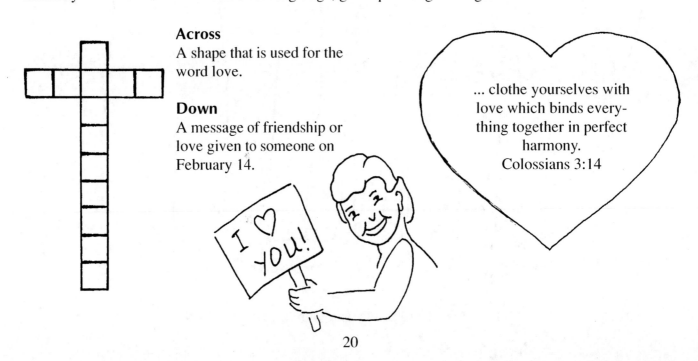

Across
A shape that is used for the word love.

Down
A message of friendship or love given to someone on February 14.

... clothe yourselves with love which binds every-thing together in perfect harmony.
Colossians 3:14

I ♥ YOU!

20

Jesus wants to be king of our hearts.

Find the underlined words in the puzzle. They will go left to right or down.

When Jesus lived, <u>donkeys</u> were a <u>favorite</u> <u>animal</u>. They could <u>carry</u> <u>people</u> and <u>heavy</u> <u>loads</u>. They <u>were</u> an animal of <u>peace</u>. Jesus <u>rode</u> a donkey into <u>Jerusalem</u>. People who had <u>heard</u> about <u>him</u> or had seen some of his <u>miracles</u> <u>met</u> him <u>shouting</u> and <u>waving</u> <u>palm</u> <u>leaves</u>. They <u>wanted</u> him to be <u>king</u>. Jesus chose to <u>die</u> for <u>us</u> instead. His death <u>on</u> the <u>cross</u> <u>shows</u> us how much he loves us. He wants to be king but only in our <u>heart</u>.

```
S  X  H  X  H  E  A  R  D  H  I  M  L
H  X  E  X  D  O  N  K  E  Y  S  I  E
O  F  A  V  O  R  I  T  E  W  H  R  A
W  A  V  I  N  G  M  U  S  A  O  A  V
S  C  Y  P  L  O  A  D  S  N  U  C  E
P  R  P  E  O  P  L  E  M  T  T  L  S
A  O  C  A  R  R  Y  O  E  E  I  E  R
L  S  X  C  D  I  E  N  T  D  N  S  O
M  S  H  E  A  R  T  K  I  N  G  X  D
J  E  R  U  S  A  L  E  M  W  E  R  E
```

Across
A donkey was thought of as an animal of _ _ _ _ _.

Down
This is the day we remember Jesus' ride into Jerusalem on a donkey. We call this day

_ _ _ _ _ _ _ _ _ _ _.

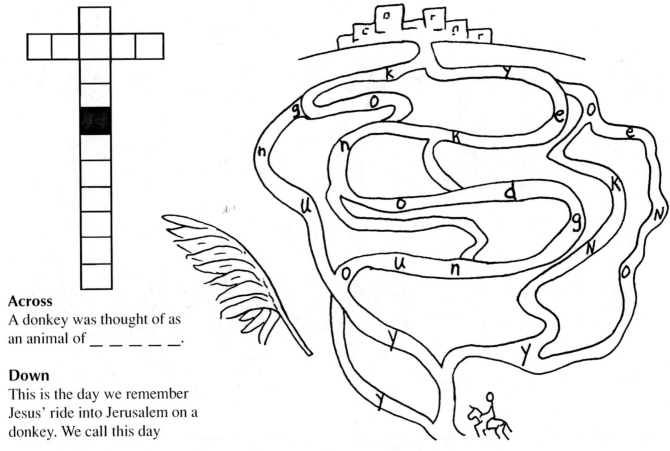

Find your way to the city. As you go, write the letters you find in the blanks below to complete the sentence.

Jesus found a _ _ _ _ _ _ _ _ _ _ _ and sat on it.

John 12:14

22

Jesus promises us eternal life.

Unscramble the words.

Easter _____ is a wonderful _____ for God's people because we celebrate the _____
udSnya   ayd   rrreseciount

of Jesus from _____ and he promised that we would have resurrection _____ if we'll _____ in
eadht   oot   iebelev

him. Seeds _____ in the ground help us understand. When seeds are planted they die, but as they
lptedan

_____ a new plant _____. Only if the seed dies will there be new life. But, the _____ Jesus promises
ied   rwogs   feli

us will be forever.

Find the words from the list in the puzzle. They will go left to right or down.

```
D  A  Y  B  E  L  I  E  V  E  H  E
L  I  F  E  U  S  T  O  O  I  F  X
O  N  J  C  I  N  X  H  I  M  P  W
C  D  E  A  T  H  M  U  S  T  R  O
R  E  S  U  R  R  E  C  T  I  O  N
O  A  U  S  S  E  E  D  S  H  M  D
S  S  S  E  E  V  E  N  D  E  I  E
S  T  S  P  R  I  N  G  I  L  S  R
C  E  L  E  B  R  A  T  E  P  E  F
F  R  O  M  L  I  V  E  T  O  S  U
U  N  D  E  R  S  T  A  N  D  X  L
```

Easter	us
is	life
wonderful	too
day	if
because	believe
celebrate	in
Jesus	him
resurrection	spring
from	seeds
death	help
on	understand
cross	must
he	die
even	to
promises	live

Across

Jesus promises us

_ _ _ _ _ _ _ _ life.

Down

Jesus promises us

_ _ _ _ _ _ _ _ _ _ _

from death if we'll
believe in him.

What does "eternal" mean? Circle the right answer.

a short time
forever
none at all

Jesus said, "I am the resurrection and the life. Those who believe in me, even though they die, will live."
John 11:25

24

Jesus asks us to serve.

Find the underlined words in the puzzle. They will go left to right or down.

Jesus' friends, the <u>disciples</u>, had an <u>argument</u> one day. Each of them wanted to be the <u>greatest</u>. When Jesus asked them what they were arguing <u>about</u>, they didn't answer because they were <u>ashamed</u> of what they had <u>been</u> doing. But, Jesus knew about their argument so he told them <u>something</u> <u>important</u>. He told them that if they wanted to <u>be</u> great, they must become a <u>servant</u>. Jesus meant someone who does things <u>for</u> others because they <u>care</u> that <u>others</u> have what they <u>need</u>. <u>Jesus</u> <u>became</u> our servant when he <u>died</u> <u>on</u> the <u>cross</u>. <u>Mothers</u> are great. One <u>reason</u> is that they <u>serve</u> us because of their <u>love</u> for <u>us</u>. Be sure to <u>thank</u> Mother for all she does.

X	S	O	M	E	T	H	I	N	G	I
B	E	C	R	O	S	S	U	S	R	M
A	R	G	U	M	E	N	T	N	E	P
B	X	R	F	O	R	X	D	E	A	O
O	C	E	L	O	V	E	I	E	S	R
U	A	A	S	H	A	M	E	D	O	T
T	R	T	H	A	N	K	D	O	N	A
B	E	E	N	O	T	H	E	R	S	N
D	I	S	C	I	P	L	E	S	X	T
M	O	T	H	E	R	S	E	R	V	E
J	E	S	U	S	B	E	C	A	M	E

Across

Jesus said that the way to become

— — — — —

Down

is to become a

— — — — — — —.

Mother serves you. Are there ways that you can serve her?
Cross out the wrong words.

Pick up my toys.

Frown about it.

Help set the table.

Pout about it.

Make my bed.

Complain about it.

Hang up my coat.

Forget about it.

Bring Mother a drink.

Smile about it.

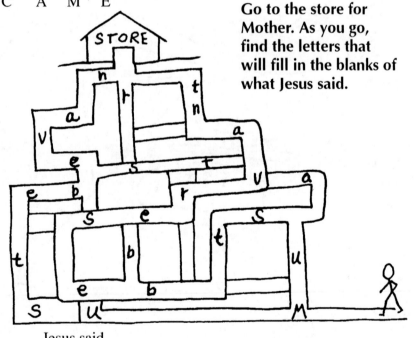

Go to the store for Mother. As you go, find the letters that will fill in the blanks of what Jesus said.

Jesus said,

"Whoever wishes to become great among you __ __ __ __ __ __ your __ __ __ __ __ __ __." Mark 10:43

We listen to Father and obey him.

Fill in the blanks to complete each word with one of the vowels, *a e i o u.*

We should h_n_r our Father every d__y of the year. One w__y to do this is to __b__y him. The Bible says we sh_ __ld pay __tt_nti_n to Father, l_st_n to wh_t he says and if we w_ll, he will te__ch __s and we will l_arn many things that we n_ __d to kn__w to become a b_tter pers_n as we grow __lder.

Find the words from the list in the puzzle. They go left to right or down.

D	O	T	R	U	T	H	F	U	L	O	V	E
J	O	H	B	E	C	O	M	E	I	X	G	H
E	L	I	E	F	M	A	N	Y	S	W	O	O
S	D	N	T	A	T	T	E	N	T	I	O	N
U	E	G	T	T	H	H	V	P	E	L	D	O
S	R	S	E	H	I	I	E	A	N	L	L	R
I	F	K	R	E	S	M	R	Y	T	H	E	N
K	I	N	D	R	D	A	Y	E	A	R	A	E
G	O	O	D	O	P	E	R	S	O	N	R	E
B	E	W	E	F	C	I	T	I	Z	E	N	D
O	B	E	Y	T	H	A	N	K	G	R	O	W

thank   then
honor   learn
father   many
every   things
day   need
of   know
year   become
do   better
this   person
obey   grow
him   older
pay   be
attention   truthful
listen   kind
if   good (2 times)
we   citizen
will   love
    Jesus

Unscramble the words and fill in the blanks.

We _____ and _____
    oelv   byeo
our _____. We
        ahtref
should _____ love and
        osla
obey our heavenly Father.

The Bible _____ "For
       ssya
the love of God is

_____, that we obey his
 sith
commandments...."

1 John 5:3

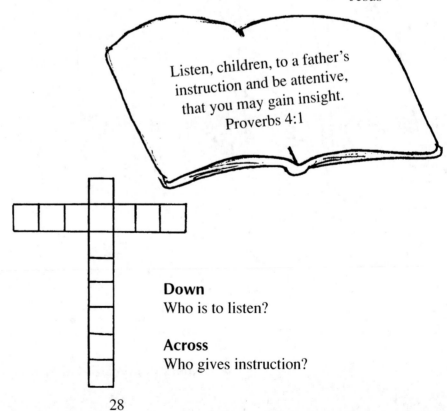

Listen, children, to a father's instruction and be attentive, that you may gain insight.
Proverbs 4:1

Down
Who is to listen?

Across
Who gives instruction?

28

We pray for our country's leaders.

The underlined words will be found in the puzzle below. They will go left to right or down.

Over 200 <u>years</u> <u>ago</u> the <u>leaders</u> of the United States <u>wrote</u> and <u>signed</u> a <u>paper</u> <u>called</u> the <u>Declaration of Independence</u>. On the <u>Fourth</u> of <u>July</u> we <u>celebrate</u> what they did and our country's freedom. <u>Those</u> leaders did a <u>good</u> job for <u>us</u>, but <u>each</u> one of us can <u>help</u> our <u>country</u>, <u>too</u>, by doing what the Bible says. It <u>says</u> <u>we</u> are to <u>pray</u> for our leaders. We <u>all</u> <u>want</u> to <u>live</u> a good, <u>peaceful</u> <u>life</u> and be <u>free</u> to <u>worship</u> God.

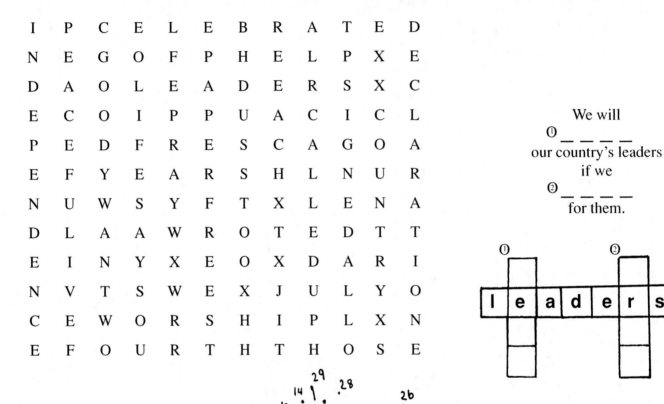

I	P	C	E	L	E	B	R	A	T	E	D
N	E	G	O	F	P	H	E	L	P	X	E
D	A	O	L	E	A	D	E	R	S	X	C
E	C	O	I	P	P	U	A	C	I	C	L
P	E	D	F	R	E	S	C	A	G	O	A
E	F	Y	E	A	R	S	H	L	N	U	R
N	U	W	S	Y	F	T	X	L	E	N	A
D	L	A	A	W	R	O	T	E	D	T	T
E	I	N	Y	X	E	O	X	D	A	R	I
N	V	T	S	W	E	X	J	U	L	Y	O
C	E	W	O	R	S	H	I	P	L	X	N
E	F	O	U	R	T	H	T	H	O	S	E

We will
① _ _ _ _
our country's leaders
if we
② _ _ _ _
for them.

① ②
l e a d e r s

The Bible in 1 Timothy 2:1-4 says that we should make supplications, prayers, intercessions, and thanksgivings for our leaders. Draw a line from the word to what you think it means.

supplications   to ask for something for someone else

prayers   to say we appreciate and are grateful for someone or something

intercessions   to talk to God

thanksgivings   to make a humble request

30

Jesus had to learn. He understands and will help.

Find the underlined words in the puzzle. They go left to right or down.

Jesus was a <u>child</u> and had to <u>grow</u> up <u>learning</u> things <u>just</u> as all of us do. <u>That</u> is <u>why</u> he <u>understands</u> how <u>hard</u> it <u>is</u> <u>for</u> <u>us</u> <u>sometimes</u>. And that is why <u>he</u> is <u>able</u> to <u>help</u> us. <u>Since</u> <u>we</u> <u>know</u> he <u>does</u> want to help we <u>can</u> <u>go</u> to <u>him</u> in our <u>prayers</u> and <u>ask</u>. Then the Bible <u>promises</u> he will help. Of course, he <u>expects</u> us to do our <u>part</u>. We <u>must</u> <u>study</u> and do the things we should to <u>learn</u>.

P	D	O	E	S	U	X	K	X	P
R	L	E	A	R	N	I	N	G	R
O	C	H	I	L	D	W	O	R	A
M	A	B	L	E	E	E	W	O	Y
I	N	X	H	A	R	D	H	W	E
S	A	G	J	U	S	T	Y	H	R
E	S	O	M	E	T	I	M	E	S
S	K	X	U	P	A	R	T	H	I
H	I	M	S	X	N	X	H	E	N
X	I	S	T	U	D	Y	A	L	C
L	E	A	R	N	S	U	T	P	E
E	X	P	E	C	T	S	F	O	R

Across

_ _ _ _ _ was once a child.

Down

He _ _ _ _ _ _ _ _ _ _ _ _ _ and will help us.

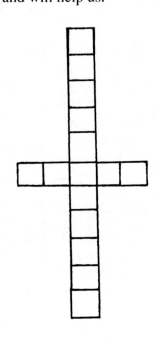

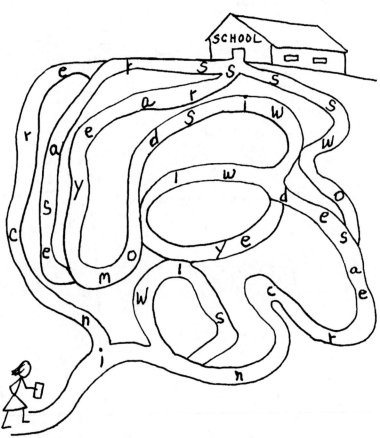

Help Sarah find her way to school. Write the letters she passes in the blanks to complete the words from Luke 2:52.

And Jesus _ _ _ _ _ _ _ _ _ _ in _ _ _ _ _ _ _ and in _ _ _ _ _ _, and in divine and human favor.

32

God keeps his promises.

Find the words in the list in the puzzle. They go left to right or down.

C	O	U	N	T	X	H	E	L	P	L	A
W	O	N	D	E	R	F	U	L	S	I	U
C	X	H	E	A	V	E	N	X	P	F	T
A	S	E	P	T	E	M	B	E	R	E	U
N	X	S	E	A	S	O	N	H	I	M	M
B	R	I	N	G	S	C	G	H	N	O	N
E	O	R	D	E	R	H	O	O	G	T	X
T	A	F	A	L	L	A	D	M	O	H	B
E	L	A	B	W	I	N	T	E	R	E	E
R	W	I	L	L	X	G	O	F	T	R	A
N	A	L	E	A	R	E	O	N	O	S	U
A	Y	P	R	O	M	I	S	E	S	I	T
L	S	U	M	M	E	R	N	O	T	N	Y
T	H	E	Y	O	U	I	T	A	N	D	X

September	dependable
brings	will
season	not
of	fail
autumn	wonderful
or	you
fall	can
it	count
change	on
to	him
winter	others
spring	too
summer	eternal
always	life
order	help
God	and
the	home
promises	in
are	heaven
beauty	

How many sentences can you make using just the words from the list?

_____

_____

_____

_____

_____

Use underlined words from Genesis 8:22 in the crossword puzzle. The words going across are marked with an *.

As long as the *earth endures, *seedtime and harvest, *cold and heat, summer and *winter, day and night, shall not cease.

Genesis 8:22

34

A mask cannot fool God. He sees what's in our heart.

Find the underlined words in the puzzle. They go left to right or down.

Sometimes our face is like a mask. We might look all right but inside our minds are busy with bad thoughts or feelings. We might even smile and still have thoughts of anger, jealousy, or hate. We can fool people who see us, but we can never fool God. He sees us on our inside. We should want our hearts and minds to look good to God. It's possible to look good to God if we take Jesus as our Savior and ask for his help.

```
S  B  W  M  A  S  K  N  G  O  O  D  J  F
H  U  E  L  O  O  K  E  H  E  L  P  E  O
O  S  S  I  F  M  B  V  A  M  A  T  A  O
U  Y  M  O  N  E  A  E  M  I  N  H  L  L
L  M  I  G  H  T  D  R  R  N  G  O  O  P
D  A  L  X  I  I  N  S  I  D  E  U  U  E
W  S  E  E  S  M  A  T  G  S  R  G  S  O
E  K  F  A  C  E  S  I  H  U  S  H  Y  P
H  E  A  R  T  S  K  L  T  H  A  T  E  L
W  A  N  T  F  E  E  L  I  N  G  S  W  E
T  A  K  E  J  E  S  U  S  A  V  I  O  R
```

Color the shapes marked X to see what is in this heart.

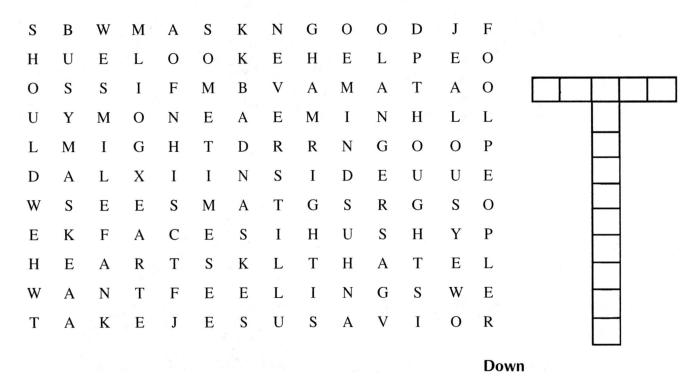

Down

People look at our outward

_ _ _ _ _ _ _ _ _ _ _.

Across

God looks at our

_ _ _ _ _.

1 Samuel 16:7

... and the Lord does not see as mortals see; they look on the outward appearance but the Lord looks on the heart. 1 Samuel 16:7b

36

Every day is a day for giving thanks.

Unscramble the words and write them in the blank places.

We have _____ Day once a _____. It is a happy _____ when _____
anhTksginvgi raye lohiayd mafiiles
get together, have fun and a lot to _____. It should _____ be a day of giving _____ to God for all
tae sola skthna
he has _____ for us. We should thank him _____ day especially for his _____ when he sent Jesus
oedn yreve veol
to die for ___.
su

Find the words from the list in the puzzle. They go left to right or down.

P	U	M	P	K	I	N	S	N	O
B	U	T	T	U	R	K	E	Y	S
L	A	X	H	O	L	I	D	A	Y
E	N	H	A	P	P	Y	A	H	S
S	D	T	N	L	N	X	Y	E	O
S	E	H	K	A	O	B	E	L	F
I	A	E	S	Y	T	W	E	P	A
N	T	O	G	E	T	H	E	R	M
G	R	T	I	M	E	W	W	T	I
S	E	Z	V	S	C	H	O	O	L
X	J	G	I	V	E	E	R	O	I
F	O	E	N	D	S	N	K	X	E
O	I	S	G	T	H	A	N	K	S
R	C	T	H	A	N	K	F	U	L
J	E	S	U	S	L	O	V	E	X

Thanksgiving	the
is	day
happy	ends
time	but
holiday	not
no	blessings
school	so
work	be
pumpkins	thankful
turkeys	we
when	rejoice
families	too
together	for
eat	Jesus
play	love
give	and
thanks	help

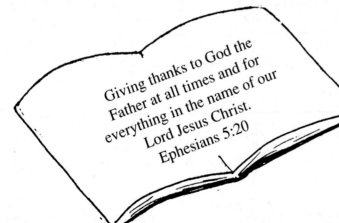

Giving thanks to God the Father at all times and for everything in the name of our Lord Jesus Christ.
Ephesians 5:20

Across

Thanksgiving is a happy

_ _ _ _ _ _ _.

Down

The Bible says we should be

_ _ _ _ _ _

_ _ _ _ _ _

to God the Father at all times.

Jesus came to show us God's love.

Find the underlined words in the puzzle below. They will go left to right or down.

We celebrate in December. It is the time we remember the birth of Jesus. Many years before Jesus was born, people knew and worshiped God. But, very few knew or understood what God is really like. One of the reasons Jesus came into our world was to show us what God is like. We can look at the life of Jesus and learn that God loves us very much and wants us to love him. He wants to be our heavenly Father and asks us to believe in Jesus and all Jesus said and did. Jesus showed us how much God loves us when he left his heavenly home to come and live on earth to die for us. We rejoice and celebrate the birth of Jesus into our world to show us what God is really like.

R	R	O	U	R	E	A	S	O	N	S	B
E	E	N	N	T	K	J	E	S	U	S	E
M	J	E	D	O	N	L	O	V	E	S	L
E	O	D	E	C	E	M	B	E	R	X	I
M	I	M	R	E	W	L	I	K	E	W	E
B	C	U	S	L	E	A	R	N	W	O	V
E	E	C	T	E	F	A	T	H	E	R	E
R	A	H	O	B	X	S	H	X	R	L	L
W	R	W	O	R	S	H	I	P	E	D	O
A	T	O	D	A	C	O	M	E	A	I	O
N	H	U	X	T	O	W	A	L	L	E	K
T	O	R	H	E	A	V	E	N	L	Y	U
S	F	D	X	L	I	V	E	R	Y	X	S

Here are some things Jesus said in John 14:7 and 9. Find words to fit the crossword puzzle. The words marked with an * go across.

"*Whoever has seen me has seen the Father."
"If you know me you will know my Father *also."

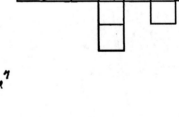

The disciples saw Jesus and spent time with him.
How can we learn about Jesus?
Unscramble the words.

_ _ _ _ _ the _ _ _ _ _ _.
  adre   elBib

_ _ _ _ _ to _ _ _ _ _ _ _.
 meco   hchcur

BIBLE

40

ANSWER KEYS

Pages 18, 20, 22

Find the underlined words in the puzzle. They will go left to right or down.

When we do our lessons or draw a picture, we can erase any mistakes we make with an eraser.

As we live each day we might do things that are wrong. God calls this sin. If we are sorry and ask God to forgive us, he will erase those things away. The Bible says that it is the blood of Jesus that cleanses us. Each day can be a new beginning.

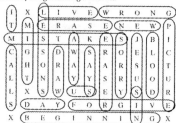

Help Bob find his way to school. Fill in the blanks with the letters he finds on his way.

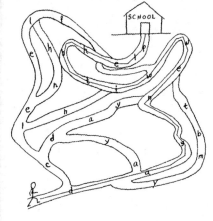

Across
Jesus shed his **b l o o d** on the cross.

Down
He did this so that our sins could be **f o r g i v e n**.

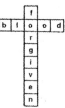

... the blood of Jesus his son cleanses us from all sin.
1 John 1:7b

Each **d a y** can be a **n e w** beginning **w i t h** God's forgiveness and **h e l p**!

18

Find the words from the list in the puzzle below. They will go down or from left to right.

valentines, have, hearts, stands, for, love (2 times), care, others, doing, well, show, compassion, kindness, humility, patience, forgive, live, harmony, binds, us (3 times), together, Jesus, wants, you, to, try (3 times), meekness

Draw a line from the word to what you think it means.

compassion — a great caring and concern for someone
kindness — to be gentle and helpful
humility — to not be proud or think yourself better than others
meekness — patient, humble, gentle, and not bossy
patience — to have trouble without complaining
forgive — don't hold a grudge, give up feelings of anger
love — to all agree and get along well with each other
harmony — sorrow for someone that is hurting

Across
A shape that is used for the word love. (heart)

Down
A message of friendship or love given to someone on February 14. (valentine)

... clothe yourselves with love which binds everything together in perfect harmony.
Colossians 3:14

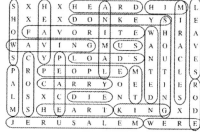

20

Find the underlined words in the puzzle. They will go left to right or down.

When Jesus lived, donkeys were a favorite animal. They could carry people and heavy loads. They were an animal of peace. Jesus rode a donkey into Jerusalem. People who had heard about him or had seen some of his miracles met him shouting and waving palm leaves. They wanted him to be king. Jesus chose to die for us instead. His death on the cross shows us how much he loves us. He wants to be king but only in our heart.

Across
A donkey was thought of as an animal of **p e a c e**.

Down
This is the day we remember Jesus' ride into Jerusalem on a donkey. We call this day **P a l m S u n d a y**.

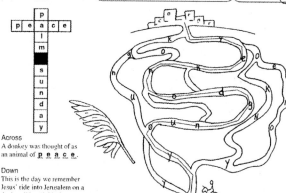

Find your way to the city. As you go, write the letters you find in the blanks below to complete the sentence.

Jesus found a **y o u n g d o n k e y** and sat on it.
John 12:14

22

ANSWER
KEYS

Pages 24, 26, 28

Unscramble the words.

Easter **Sunday** is a wonderful **day** for God's people because we celebrate the **resurrection**
of Jesus from **death** and he promised that we would have resurrection **too** if we'll **believe** in
him. Seeds **planted** in the ground help us understand. When seeds are planted they die, but as they
die a new plant **grows** . Only if the seed dies will there be new life. But, the **life** Jesus promises
us will be forever.

Find the words from the list in the puzzle. They will go left to right or down.

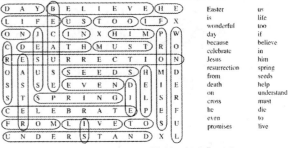

D	A	Y	B	E	L	I	E	V	E	(H)	E	
L	I	F	E	U	S	T	O	O	I	F	X	
O	N	J	C	I	N	X	H	I	M	P	W	
C	D	E	A	T	H	M	U	S	T	R	O	
R	E	S	U	R	R	E	C	T	I	O	N	
O	A	U	S	S	E	E	D	S	H	M	D	
S	S	S	E	V	E	N	D	E	L	I	E	
S	T	S	P	R	I	N	G	I	L	S	R	
C	E	L	E	B	R	A	T	E	P	E	F	
F	R	O	M	L	I	V	E	T	O	S	U	
U	N	D	E	R	S	T	A	N	D	X	L	

Easter	us
is	life
wonderful	too
day	if
because	believe
celebrate	in
Jesus	him
resurrection	spring
from	seeds
death	help
on	understand
cross	must
he	die
even	to
promises	live

What does "eternal" mean?
Circle the right answer.

Across

Jesus promises us
e t e r n a l life.

a short time
(forever)
none at all

Down

Jesus promises us
r e s u r r e c t i o n
from death if we'll
believe in him.

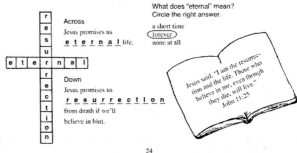

Jesus said, "I am the resurrection and the life. Those who believe in me, even though they die, will live."
John 11:25

24

Find the underlined words in the puzzle. They will go left to right or down.

Jesus' friends, the <u>disciples</u>, had an <u>argument</u> one day. Each of them wanted to be the <u>greatest</u>. When Jesus
asked them what they were arguing <u>about</u>, they didn't answer because they were <u>ashamed</u> of what they had
<u>been</u> doing. But, Jesus knew about their argument so he told them <u>something important</u>. He told them that
if they wanted to <u>be</u> great, they must become a <u>servant</u>. Jesus meant someone who does things <u>for</u> others
because they <u>care</u> that <u>others</u> have what they <u>need</u>. <u>Jesus became</u> our servant when he <u>died on the cross</u>.
<u>Mothers</u> are great. One <u>reason</u> is that they <u>serve</u> us because of their <u>love</u> for us. Be sure to <u>thank</u> Mother for
all she does.

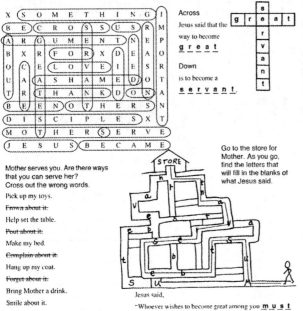

X	S	O	M	E	T	H	I	N	G	J	M
B	E	C	R	O	S	S	U	S	R	P	
A	R	G	U	M	E	N	T	N	E	R	
B	X	R	F	O	R	X	D	E	A	S	
O	U	C	L	O	V	E	I	E	T	
U	A	A	S	H	A	M	E	D	O	T	
T	R	T	H	A	N	K	D	O	N	A	
B	E	E	N	O	T	H	E	R	S	N	
D	I	S	C	I	P	L	E	S	X	T	
M	O	T	H	E	R	S	E	R	V	E	
J	E	S	U	S	B	E	C	A	M	E	

Across
Jesus said that the
way to become
g r e a t

Down
is to become a
s e r v a n t

(crossword)
g r e a t
s
e
r
v
a
n
t

Mother serves you. Are there ways
that you can serve her?
Cross out the wrong words.

Pick up my toys.
~~Frown about it.~~
Help set the table.
~~Pout about it.~~
Make my bed.
~~Complain about it.~~
Hang up my coat.
~~Forget about it.~~
Bring Mother a drink.
Smile about it.

Go to the store for
Mother. As you go,
find the letters that
will fill in the blanks of
what Jesus said.

Jesus said,
"Whoever wishes to become great among you **m u s t**
b e your **s e r v a n t**." Mark 10:43

26

Fill in the blanks to complete each word with one of the vowels, a e i o u.

We should h**o**n**o**r our Father every d**a**y of the year. One w**a**y to do this is to **o**b**e**y him. The Bible says
we sh**o****u**ld pay **a**tt**e**nt**i**on to Father, l**i**st**e**n to wh**a**t he says and if we w**i**ll, he will te**a**ch **e**s and we
will le**a**rn many things that we n**e**ed to kn**o**w to become a b**e**tter p**e**rs**o**n as we grow **o**lder.

Find the words from the list in the puzzle. They go left to right or down.

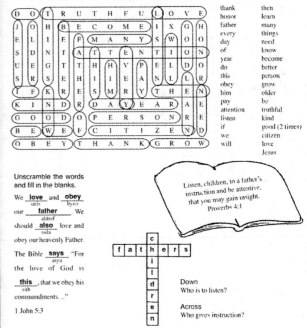

D	O	T	R	U	T	H	F	U	L	O	V	E	
J	O	H	B	E	C	O	M	E	I	X	G	O	
E	L	I	E	F	M	A	N	Y	S	W	O	O	
S	D	H	T	A	T	T	E	N	T	I	O	N	
U	E	G	T	H	H	Y	P	E	L	D	O	
S	R	S	E	H	I	I	E	A	N	L	L	R	
T	F	K	R	E	S	M	R	Y	T	H	E	N	
K	I	N	D	R	D	A	Y	E	A	R	A	E	
G	O	O	D	O	P	E	R	S	O	N	R	E	
B	E	W	E	F	C	I	T	I	Z	E	N	D	
O	B	E	Y	T	H	A	N	K	G	R	O	W	

thank	then
honor	learn
father	many
every	things
day	need
of	know
year	become
do	better
this	person
obey	grow
him	older
pay	be
attention	truthful
listen	kind
if	good (2 times)
we	citizen
will	love
	Jesus

Unscramble the words
and fill in the blanks.

We **love** and **obey**
our **father** . We
should **also** love and
obey our heavenly Father.

The Bible **says** "For
the love of God is
this , that we obey his
commandments. .."

1 John 5:3

Listen, children, to a father's
instruction and be attentive,
that you may gain insight.
Proverbs 4:1

(crossword)
f a t h e r s
c
h
i
l
d
r
e
n

Down
Who is to listen?

Across
Who gives instruction?

28

ANSWER KEYS
Pages 30, 32, 34

The underlined words will be found in the puzzle below. They will go left to right or down.

Over 200 years ago the leaders of the United States wrote and signed a paper called the Declaration of Independence. On the Fourth of July we celebrate what they did and our country's freedom. Those leaders did a good job for us, but each one of us can help our country, too, by doing what the Bible says. It says we are to pray for our leaders. We all want to live a good, peaceful life and be free to worship God.

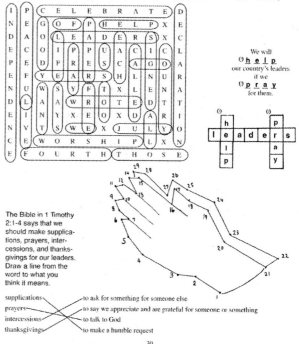

We will
ⓞ **h e l p**
our country's leaders
if we
ⓞ **p r a y**
for them.

The Bible in 1 Timothy 2:1-4 says that we should make supplications, prayers, intercessions, and thanksgivings for our leaders. Draw a line from the word to what you think it means.

supplications — to ask for something for someone else
prayers — to say we appreciate and are grateful for someone or something
intercessions — to talk to God
thanksgivings — to make a humble request

30

Find the underlined words in the puzzle. They go left to right or down.

Jesus was a child and had to grow up learning things just as all of us do. That is why he understands how hard it is for us sometimes. And that is why he is able to help us. Since we know he does want to help we can go to him in our prayers and ask. Then the Bible promises he will help. Of course, he expects us to do our part. We must study and do the things we should to learn.

Across
J e s u s was once a child.

Down
He **u n d e r s t a n d s**
and will help us.

```
        u
        n
        d
        e
        r
J e s u s
        t
        a
        n
        d
        s
```

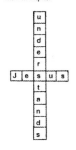

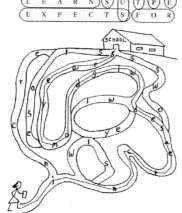

Help Sarah find her way to school. Write the letters she passes in the blanks to complete the words from Luke 2:52.

And Jesus **i n c r e a s e d** in **w i s d o m** and in **y e a r s**, and in divine and human favor.

32

Find the words in the list in the puzzle. They go left to right or down.

September	dependable
brings	will
season	not
of	fail
autumn	wonderful
or	you
fall	can
it	count
change	on
to	him
winter	others
spring	too
summer	eternal
always	life
order	help
God	and
the	home
promises	in
are	heaven
beauty	

How many sentences can you make using just the words from the list?

_____

_____

_____

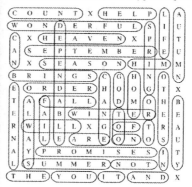

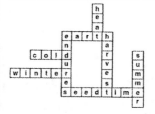

Use underlined words from Genesis 8:22 in the crossword puzzle. The words going across are marked with an *.

As long as the *earth endures, *seedtime and harvest, *cold and heat, summer and *winter, day and night, shall not cease.

Genesis 8:22

34

43

ANSWER KEYS

Pages 36, 38, 40

Find the underlined words in the puzzle. They go left to right or down.

Sometimes our face is like a mask. We might look all right but inside our minds are busy with bad thoughts or feelings. We might even smile and still have thoughts of anger, jealousy, or hate. We can fool people who see us, but we can never fool God. He sees us on our inside. We should want our hearts and minds to look good to God. It's possible to look good to God if we take Jesus as our Savior and ask for his help.

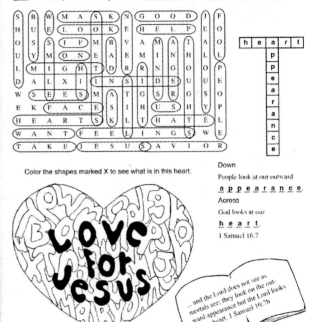

Color the shapes marked X to see what is in this heart.

Down

People look at our outward

a p p e a r a n c e.

Across

God looks at our

h e a r t.

1 Samuel 16:7

...and the Lord does not see as mortals see; they look on the outward appearance but the Lord looks on the heart. 1 Samuel 16:7b

36

Unscramble the words and write them in the blank places.

We have **Thanksgiving** Day once a **year**. It is a happy **holiday** when **families**
anhTksgiivgi / raye / lohiayd / mafilies
get together, have fun and a lot to **eat**. It should **also** be a day of giving **thanks** to God for all
tae / sola / skthna
he has **done** for us. We should thank him **every** day especially for his **love** when he sent Jesus
oedn / yréve / veol
to die for **us**.
su

Find the words from the list in the puzzle. They go left to right or down.

Thanksgiving — the
is — day
happy — ends
time — but
holiday — not
no — blessings
school — so
work — be
pumpkins — thankful
turkeys — we
when — rejoice
families — too
together — for
eat — Jesus
play — love
give — and
thanks — help

Across

Thanksgiving is a happy
h o l i d a y

Down

The Bible says we should be
g i v i n g
t h a n k s
to God the Father at all times.

Giving thanks to God the Father at all times and for everything in the name of our Lord Jesus Christ. Ephesians 5:20

38

Find the underlined words in the puzzle below. They will go left to right or down.

We celebrate in December. It is the time we remember the birth of Jesus. Many years before Jesus was born, people knew and worshiped God. But, very few knew or understood what God is really like. One of the reasons Jesus came into our world was to show us what God is like. We can look at the life of Jesus and learn that God loves us very much and wants us to love him. He wants to be our heavenly Father and asks us to believe in Jesus and all Jesus said and did. Jesus showed us how much God loves us when he left his heavenly home to come and live on earth to die for us. We rejoice and celebrate the birth of Jesus into our world to show us what God is really like.

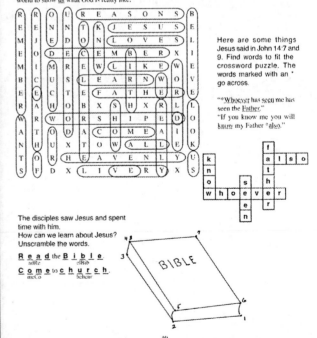

Here are some things Jesus said in John 14:7 and 9. Find words to fit the crossword puzzle. The words marked with an * go across.

"*Whoever has seen me has seen the Father."
"If you know me you will know my Father *also."

The disciples saw Jesus and spent time with him.
How can we learn about Jesus?
Unscramble the words.

R e a d the **B i b l e**.
adRe / efBib

C o m e to **c h u r c h**.
meCo / hchcur

BIBLE

40

44